# Coaching illustrated™

## a proven approach to real-world management

### by MARK DAVID

Published by The Mark David Corporation

411 Borel Avenue, Suite 504

San Mateo CA 94402

800-410-(ANSR) 2677

REALWORLD

Library of Congress Catalog Card Number 98-93996

ISBN# 1-893778-00-2

Printed in U.S.A.

illustration: Vivian Lai

art direction: Suzi McKee

editorial: Denise Crevin, Deme Jamson, Richard Fellner

photographer: Hjalmar Nilsen

# Dedication

**To my brother, Scott,**

in admiration of his courageous and heroic attitude toward life and his outstanding skills as a leader, manager and coach at Lucent Technologies.

Scott, you taught me how important it is to make a difference in everything you do and to positively impact everyone with whom you come in contact. Being by your side during your two separate battles with cancer taught me more than you'll ever know.

Not only did you teach me to appreciate life, you also allowed me to help coach you through your illnesses. I consider that the most rewarding coaching experience I have ever had and can't thank you enough for inspiring me to share my skills as a coach with others. You are a true hero.

**A special thanks to Deme Jamson for your constant support.**

Your courage, honesty, common sense and drive have enabled us to achieve our publishing dream.

You are truly amazing!

## Introduction

The most important assets of any company are the people who work there. And that's why the job of a coach is especially important. You're the one who grows and develops these people who, in turn, enable the company to grow and develop. I wrote this book to support you in improving your coaching skills and being more effective at what you do. Great coaches are not born; rather, they must learn and develop over time.

I developed my coaching skills in the business world as a turnaround expert. In that capacity, I coached both individuals and companies to increased productivity and profits. So, while coaching is now the preferred management method in Corporate America, I've been doing it for years to achieve consistent, increased results. I was ahead of the trend then and I'm ahead of the trend now. The value of this book is that it comes straight from the field. It helps you deal with what you are experiencing right now. Even more important, it makes learning this information simple.

## Introduction (cont.)

Coaching Illustrated presents 30 basic principles of successful coaching which will establish a sound foundation for any manager. It has been proven that visualization helps learning and goal achievement. Therefore, I've provided a definition and real-world example along with a picture for each principle. This way, you can learn, understand and implement in one breath!

My own research has shown time and time again that this methodology works. By using pictures, we dissolve the learning curve so you can learn new skills easily. Every manager needs this book... both for working with your team and for training less-experienced managers. We know your time is valuable — this book will help guide you to increased success and job satisfaction quickly and easily.

Oh, one more thing. You may have noticed the little cartoon character with me at the top of the previous page. You'll be seeing a lot of this cartoon character, so I'd like to properly introduce you. This icon represents you. So, picture yourself implementing the coaching tips I've outlined for you and see yourself being a true coach for your team. Good luck and enjoy!

*Mark David*

P.S. Try sharing these 30 coaching principles with your family. I've taught them to my wife and two children. It's made a positive difference in our lives. I'm sure it will in yours as well!

# Table of Contents

# Table of Contents

# #1 BROADCAST
## your Vision to the team

Winning coaches start each "season" with a Vision in mind. Make sure your Vision is defined and presented for everyone to understand. Your Vision then becomes the Vision of the team. The key to getting your team to understand your Vision clearly is for it to be communicated often: on a daily, weekly, monthly and quarterly basis. When people refer to everyone being on the same page, it means that everyone understands the team Vision and his/her part in achieving it. This conditioning is extremely motivating and is the core of building a high-performance team.

Broadcast your Vision by pre-planning a quarterly marketing campaign. Here are some ways to implement your campaign:
1. Leave voice mails reiterating the Vision and update team members on their progress toward achieving it. Congratulate them on their efforts and challenge them further.
2. E-mail information with team members' successes and current events that relate to the Vision.
3. Create a monthly newsletter that refocuses the team on the Vision — recognizing outstanding contributions, sacrifices, etc.
4. Interview customers and create audio/video recordings to share with the team. This gives your team members a larger scope to which they can relate their efforts.
5. Schedule regular team meetings to discuss the Vision and each team member's efforts toward achieving it.

**example**

A manager of a small company was building a team that would take the company to its next level. Her Vision was to build a high-performance team that would double the size of the company and allow it to hit $1 million in revenue. She composed a slogan for her Vision: "Creating Together What We Can't Create Alone."

To broadcast her Vision to the team, she held a team meeting where she described the Vision and how the role of each team member impacted it. She made a poster with a puzzle graphic to further illustrate her Vision. Each puzzle piece represented the unique talents of each team member — illustrating how they fit together to achieve the Vision. She also designed sweatshirts with the puzzle graphic and slogan on it.

All memos after that point included the puzzle graphic. As the team grew, pieces were added to the puzzle. She also designed activities for team meetings that increased the team's awareness of the Vision. The team understood the Vision and supported it since it was broadcasted clearly and often in creative, fun and innovative ways.

## *the key to being a great coach is...*
# TRUTH!!!

Influential coaches embrace honesty as the foundation upon which their teams are built. Honesty is what enables you to lead your team forward and achieve desired goals. Truth unlocks potential, and is what you need to inspire and develop each team member.

As the team's coach, lead by example. Don't overpromise, exaggerate or speak before you have all the facts. It is important to forewarn team members of the consequences of dishonesty. The truth then becomes a shared standard of performance that must be upheld. It acts as a guiding principle that holds the team together through challenging situations.

A General Manager told his second-in-command, Laura, that she was his highest-paid employee and an extremely valuable asset to the team. Laura enjoyed her role, appreciated his support of her hard work, and acted as his advocate.

Zach, another person on the management team, was leaving the company. At his going away party, he and Laura casually began talking about the company and his future plans. They ended up discussing salaries, and Zach revealed that his current salary was higher than hers. Though the salary difference was minimal, Laura realized that the GM had not been telling her the truth. She then doubted the depth of her relationship with the GM and his motivation for lying about something so small. This reality moved her into an adversarial relationship with the GM. She started an internal campaign to get the GM removed.

Although the lie he told Laura was minor, it cost him his team member's trust, his integrity and, ultimately, his position as GM. He learned two critical rules of effective coaching that everyone should master:
1. Always tell the truth.
2. Team members <u>do</u> talk to others about matters they discuss with management.

# 3  build TRUST & RESPECT, not popularity

Never seek popularity as a coach – you will only lose. Instead, you must learn to lead your team in a manner that gains respect.

Your team members want to follow a strong leader, not a "yes" person. They also want to follow someone who operates based on what's best for the company rather than what's best for themselves or specific people. When you respect yourself and others, you build trust in your ability to manage all team members fairly.

Team members must trust their leaders or the organization will be filled with conflict. Lack of trust and respect leads to division within the company and lack of alignment with management. The bottom line of building a solid team or company is gaining trust and respect.

## example

Howard, the Vice President of a company that was being sold, noticed that the team's productivity had decreased dramatically since the announcement of the sale. The team met and found they had lost focus because they were afraid of what would happen to their jobs after the sale. The popular thing would have been to join them in their feelings, succumb to a shared mental strike and boycott the work because of the unknown.

As the team's leader, Howard decided to keep the team focused on its present goals. He called mandatory 8 a.m. meetings every day and "drilled for skill" with team members. These "drills" focused the team on improving their performance vs. the fear of losing their jobs. This made him very unpopular because nobody wanted to come to these meetings or participate. They preferred to be "victims" of the company being sold.

However, after a month of these meetings, the team regained their focus — meeting and exceeding their goals. The quarter ended up being the most productive Howard had experienced. As team members graciously received their bonuses, the sale of the company dissolved. Although his decision was unpopular at the time, he regained the trust and respect of the team. The key to coaching individuals to their highest level is to lead through chaos, not fall victim to it.

# 4 SPEND TIME
## with your high-performers

Time constraints on today's managers make it physically impossible to spend an equal amount of time with every team member. Due to downsizing, most coaches are doing the work of two or three people. Therefore, a good strategy is to spend the time you do have with the individuals who will give you the greatest return.

Certain types of relationships will naturally unfold with team members and yourself. High-performers usually represent twenty to thirty percent of your team. These team members guarantee a better return on the time you invest in them. They model the type of behavior you desire from the rest of the team. These team members attract other high-performers — they are the individuals who establish your company's reputation and give you your competitive edge. Basically, they set the standard of performance for your entire team.

Marginal players do the opposite. They pull team members down and allow mediocrity. A common mistake coaches make is to spend too much time with marginal players and not enough time with their high-performers. Marginal performers need to be quickly converted into effective, consistent high-performers through group and individual training. This training opens the door for them to succeed at a higher level. If they don't accomplish what is needed to improve, they must be de-hired. It is the job of the coach to set the standard of excellence within a high-performance team so that everyone is motivated to succeed.

■ ■ ■ ■ **example**

Jim, a Sales Manager hired a new employee, Max, with whom he had a lot in common. Shortly after Max joined the team, the entire team's morale, sales and productivity began dropping steadily. Max was a marginal performer and was compromising the infrastructure of the team. Max was taxing Jim's time and not executing anything he was being taught. Instead, he was trying to bring everyone down to his level so he wouldn't stand out as a poor performer. Since Jim and Max had become friends, Jim had lost his objectivity and couldn't see the reality of the situation.

One day, Jim walked past the conference room and heard Max talking negatively about the company and one of its new products to two of Jim's top performers. He immediately set up a meeting with Max and confronted him about his behavior. Max denied everything, but he agreed to leave the company.

After the announcement of Max's departure, Jim's team members lined up outside his door waiting to ask the same questions: "What took you so long? Why didn't you get rid of him sooner? Why did you stop giving us your time? Do you realize how much that affected our motivation?" Jim realized that good coaches take care of their high-performers, help marginal performers improve and guide the rest to find new careers before they ruin the team.

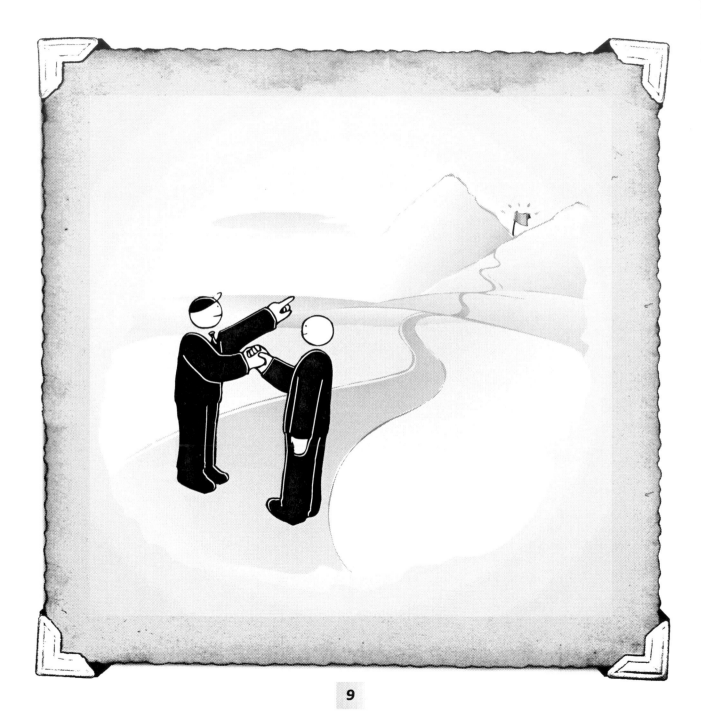

# 5 *build strong* LONG-TERM PARTNERSHIPS

Successful coaches build long-term partnerships with their team members. This relationship allows the coach and each team member to work together and build processes that will take them to the next level. Strong partnerships give everyone a feeling of security. As you build long-term partnerships with each team member, you create a reputation for making people a priority. Strong partnerships develop over long periods of time and include periods of conflict, challenge and fun. Learning from each other during both good times and bad times is what strengthens the relationship.

Here are some key components of building long-term partnerships:
* Share a common Vision that is reviewed as often as possible.
* Define each person's role in the partnership.
* Understand each other's strengths and weaknesses — Long-term partnerships are based on compromise and acceptance.
* Expect honesty and don't settle for anything less.
* Enjoy each other and have fun! Humor helps to hold the partnership together.
* Make sure each person invests equal time in the partnership. The more time each person gives, the stronger the partnership will become.

■ ■ ■ ■ **example**

A Fortune 50 company acquired a small business and dramatically changed its culture. The small company went from a family-oriented environment to a centralized operation run by unfamiliar leaders. Many of the original employees became unhappy and questioned their future in this new environment.

The company's president realized he needed to focus on building long-term partnerships to decrease the turnover that usually results from an acquisition. He communicated his Vision for the company and mentioned foreseen obstacles on the road. He acknowledged there would be continuous change along the way and expressed his desire to work together as a team and learn from each other's successes and failures.

In a short period of time, half of the original team members decided these changes were not for them and moved on. The remaining team members believed in the Vision and new leadership, and were willing to work together to reach the opportunities on the horizon. These individuals formed a long-term partnership with the new organization and moved up the corporate ladder. In fact, three of them now hold the company's top positions in the areas of income and level of responsibility. Their positions improved largely because they stayed and realized the value of building long-term partnerships.

# Review #1 — #5

Though these coaching tips are familiar, the key is to learn, understand and internalize each of them. They should become an automatic and permanent part of your professional behavior. We've included the following review activity to help you.

First, identify the principle that corresponds to each illustration. Then, think about how you have used this principle in the past, or come up with a plan to put it into action in the future. This type of reflection activity will help you master each principle and easily implement it in your world. Have fun!

# \_\_\_\_ _____

_____

**Action:** _____

_____

_____

_____

# \_\_\_\_ _____

_____

**Action:** _____

_____

_____

_____

\# \_\_\_\_ _____

_____

**Action:** _____

_____

_____

_____

\# \_\_\_\_ _____

_____

**Action:** _____

_____

_____

_____

\# \_\_\_\_ _____

_____

**Action:** _____

_____

_____

_____

# #6 BELIEVE *big*

Most people that work for you will concentrate only on their specific job. Though this focus is critical to the company's success, it is even more important for each team member to have the ability to "believe big."

Coach your team to "believe big" by:

1. Understanding that to "believe big" you must first "think big."
2. Understanding that it's the emotion behind the thought that creates daily miracles.
3. Asking the right questions that place emotion behind a desired thought, idea or goal. Questions such as: Why do I want to achieve this? Why is it important to me? How will I feel if I accomplish this?

By teaching your team to "believe big," you release the creativity and innovation within your entire organization. You also increase your ability to exceed your goals and "connect" your team through the sharing of ideas.

**example**

Kristen, a sales professional, was working for a small, regional, privately-held company whose average sale was around $25,000. After several months in her position, she noticed that there were several large, national companies in the same industry that were increasing their profits considerably. They did this by licensing their products. She felt that her company could compete despite its size and marketshare. She decided to break the mold of her company's current strategy by taking a risk and "believing big."

After researching, she found an industry standard formula for calculating a licensing agreement. She created a sales presentation from scratch. She practiced it until she could deliver it flawlessly. Kristen also met with her manager to rework and refine the figures and confirm his support. Once she was ready, she presented the proposal to a high-profile account targeted for this sale. The company signed the deal. Kristen had landed her company's first big-money deal — all because she never stopped "believing big."

# *tell your team*
# WHAT YOU EXPECT

Never assume that your team members know what you are thinking. As basic as it sounds, you must tell them what you expect. Be specific. You can light the path they need to take by providing clear direction. Tell them how you expect them to perform their jobs. Also, provide the action steps they need to take in order to reach their goals. State your expectations in a positive manner — if you focus on the negative, that is all the team will hear.

Setting clear expectations from the beginning prevents employee turnover. During the hiring process, provide candidates with a clear Job Description outlining the daily activities expected of them. Once hired, tell them what is expected during the first 90 days. Also, outline the skills they need to reach their next level in their career path.

Once you think they've got it, ask for feedback. If necessary, review the expectations again. The clearer the expectation, the greater the release of human potential. If your team members know what you expect, they will focus all of their energy, emotion, and intelligence into performing up to your expectations. This concentrated effort is what enables your team to do more in less time.

Tom was an extremely smart and well-educated manager, yet his team was doing poorly. A consultant was hired to improve the performance of Tom's failing team. After several meetings, the consultant realized that Tom failed to tell his team what he expected them to do on a regular basis. Tom had handed out goals at the start of each year but had only reviewed them with the team when things were behind schedule.

The consultant asked him, "Why don't you discuss these expectations with your team more often?" Tom replied, "They are intelligent, mature adults and I treat them accordingly. They should know what is expected of them just as I know what is expected of me. Besides, reviewing expectations all the time would be condescending, and I don't have the time to micromanage my people."

The consultant recommended that Tom go back to the basics. She explained that her interviews with team members uncovered that they respect Tom and want to do a good job for him. The only thing missing was his ability to communicate his expectations clearly and concisely on a regular basis. He took her advice and within 90 days the team began to improve. Tom realized that it doesn't matter how experienced or intelligent a person is; everyone needs (and wants!) direction and immediate feedback. He also realized that an effective coach needs to provide feedback regularly in order to create a high-performance team.

# 8 explain to your team WHY things must be done

**Why = Understanding = Maximum Effort = Increased Results.**

The more your team understands WHY something needs to be done, the more motivated they are to perform the activity. Take the time to explain WHY to your team members. This provides them with stability, enables you to obtain their buy-in and demonstrates your respect for them. It also increases the speed with which actions are performed. It ignites questions that can be addressed immediately.

Explaining WHY shows the team that you are interested in teaching them. This is important because it empowers them, builds loyalty and broadens their understanding of the business. It also gives each team member a better base from which to make decisions.

Explaining to your team members WHY things must be done is a habit that leads to positive outcomes. If you are giving someone a very important task, take an extra moment to confirm their understanding of the project and to obtain their feedback. This will prevent mistakes and save you many stress-filled hours in the future.

■ ■ ■ ■ **example**

A top Sales Professional needed a proposal typed for an important prospect. On the way out to lunch, he told the sales assistant to complete it for him within the hour. He simply dropped it on her desk and barked out his request without asking about <u>her</u> workload for the afternoon.

Shortly after, the lowest-performing Sales Professional came to the assistant and asked her to type a proposal for him. He explained WHY he needed it done as soon as possible and described the importance of getting it out for him. She immediately placed his proposal to the top of her list since he had taken the time to inform her of the urgency of the task.

Explaining WHY made a huge difference in this situation. The lowest-performing Sales Professional was able to make a sale and formed a positive relationship with the sales assistant that continued to pay off in the future. The top Sales Professional's sale was compromised since the proposal he needed wasn't finished within his time line.

# 9 HA, **HA**, HA
## (Hold Accountable)

Taking responsibility for your actions is no laughing matter. It's the coach's responsibility to communicate expectations to the team. All effective coaches possess the ability to hold their team members accountable for achieving agreed-upon goals. They communicate upfront the consequences of not achieving these goals. Your team members need to know that when they agree to do something, you will hold them accountable. This acts as a form of proactive motivation. It provides security because your team members always know what you expect from them and where they stand with you.

Holding team members accountable takes courage. It requires that you confront employees who are not meeting goals/expectations. By doing so, your team members will learn to inform you as early as possible when they realize a goal will not be met.

The coach that holds his team members accountable in a caring, honest and supportive atmosphere will develop a high-performance team. It is especially important that you hold everyone equally accountable. Once you allow anyone to go below your agreed-upon expectations, everyone will test the boundaries. Holding all team members equally accountable sets a consistent standard of performance.

**example**

A Vice President took over a company that was $1.5 million dollars in the red. He was hired to turn the company around quickly — which included bringing in a positive cash flow so it could go public or be sold. In reviewing the situation, he noticed that one Sales Manager, Rich, was consistently underperforming.

The company's owner was extremely close with Rich which prevented him from maintaining objectivity and holding Rich accountable. The new Vice President gave Rich a verbal warning. He explained what Rich needed to do to be successful in his position. They discussed, and agreed on, the expected results.

Not surprisingly, Rich made some mistakes. The Vice President now implemented a written corrective action plan. Rich was alarmed — he was accustomed to the owner verbally setting expectations but not following through to ensure they were met. From that point on, Rich understood the importance of reaching agreed-upon expectations. He continued to work for the Vice President. The Vice President's commitment to holding team members accountable led to the creation of a high-performance team. As a result, the company was able to go public.

# #10 *be* **PROACTIVE**, *not reactive*

The foundation of success is proactive thinking. Proactive thinking allows you to plan and create your future today.

Inspirational coaches model proactive behavior through the way they lead and manage. Teach your team members to connect today with their future by "looking ahead to get ahead." Motivate your team to look for opportunities before they become obvious in order to control their destiny.

Teach them how to prioritize their activities on a daily, weekly, monthly, quarterly and yearly basis. By aligning their activities with their goals, they will reach success more quickly.

■ ■ ■ ■ ***example***

In the 1980's, a General Manager, Jerry, took over a failing company. In the previous year, there had been a succession of three General Managers who had failed to implement successful turn-around plans. Jerry surveyed the organization and decided to utilize a proactive approach. He scheduled a company-wide meeting at the end of his second week. His primary goal was to gain the confidence of his employees and get the company back on the winning track.

Jerry created four charts to share with the team. On the first one, he shared his long range goals to be achieved in five months. On the second chart, he shared proactive steps for achieving the desired goals by the end of the five months. On the third and fourth charts, he listed his detailed plan for the first and second 30-day periods.

He went through each plan with them and showed how each connected with the other and how every employee would be held accountable. He distributed copies of each chart and asked for feedback within the week on how the plans could be improved. He then turned to an employee near the front of the room and asked, "Do you believe that <u>we</u> can do what I just shared with you?" The man smiled at Jerry and said, "Yes, because you're the only person who has provided us with a plan for the future, asked for our input and emphasized that we will all be held accountable."

Jerry's proactive approach energized the team. The five-month goal was accomplished in only three months and the company was well on its way to success.

# Review #6 — #10

Though these coaching tips are familiar, the key is to learn, understand and internalize each of them. They should become an automatic and permanent part of your professional behavior. We've included the following review activity to help you.

First, identify the principle that corresponds to each illustration. Then, think about how you have used this principle in the past, or come up with a plan to put it into action in the future. This type of reflection activity will help you master each principle and easily implement it in your world. Have fun!

# _____ _____

_____

Action: _____

_____

_____

_____

# _____ _____

_____

Action: _____

_____

_____

_____

\# \_\_\_\_\_ _____

_____

**Action:** _____

_____

_____

_____

\# \_\_\_\_\_ _____

_____

**Action:** _____

_____

_____

_____

\# \_\_\_\_\_ _____

_____

**Action:** _____

_____

_____

_____

# **11** *focus on your* **TOP 20%** *responsibilities*

One of the biggest problems in business today is lack of time. Your success depends on your ability to consistently make the choice of how to efficiently spend your time. Your Top 20% Responsibilities are the main areas of responsibility that bring you the greatest results on a daily basis. Staying focused on these areas will enable you to meet and exceed your goals. In fact, you should program your Top 20% into your subconscious so that an internal alarm goes off every time you are not focusing on them.

This type of focus is the key to mastering time management. Your Top 20% keep you on track and prevent you from falling into activity traps that are time wasters. If you were to assign a value to each of your responsibilities, your Top 20% would earn you $100 an hour while your activity traps (or low-payoff activities) would be worth just $5, $10 or $20 an hour. So, every time you perform one of these activities during the day, you are losing between $80 and $95/hr.

To be a successful coach, your Top 20% Responsibilities should include Strategic Thinking, Creating a Proactive Culture, Communication, Growing and Developing Your Team Members and Prospecting for Future Employees. Remember to take time each evening to pre-plan the next day and be sure to schedule a majority of your time on your Top 20% Responsibilities. This will ensure that you maximize your time every day.

■ ■ ■ ■ **example**

George was really excited to be part of Helen Smith's team of managers. Helen was known as a great developer of people and George was looking for a way to improve his performance. He felt he was working as hard as everyone else was, yet he was still the lowest-producing manager on the team.

During their first One-on-One meeting together, Helen said, "George, I know you are a hard worker so I am not sure why your productivity is so low. Do you have any ideas?" George replied, "No. I was actually hoping you could help me in that area." Helen said she would, and asked him two questions:

1. What are the goals and objectives the company expects you to meet?
2. What are the activities you need to be doing to achieve these goals?

She then helped George break down these activities into four headings that outlined his main areas of responsibility (Top 20%). Next, she asked George to take out his daily planner. They trended his activities over the past three months. George realized he was spending very little time with his Top 20% Responsibilities and too much time in areas that wouldn't help him achieve his overall goals. Helen stressed that it wasn't simply a matter of working hard, but a matter of focusing the majority of his time on the right activities. George took this advice and has become a consistent performer.

# #12 be an excellent DECISION MAKER

Should you or shouldn't you? Yes or no? Now or later? Skillful coaches need to be able to continually make quick and effective decisions. As a coach, you must always consider how each decision will affect individual team members and the team as a whole.

In a perfect world, you would have all the time you need to make a decision. In reality, decisions must be made quickly — based on the information that is available. Often, it's like shooting arrows at different targets. Just remember that the more you execute, the better your aim becomes. When you have to make fast decisions, listen to your instincts; if you're right 51% of the time, you're doing better than most. Be fearless in your decision-making; if you make the wrong decision, all you have to do is make the necessary adjustments.

Your goal should be to teach your team to be excellent decision-makers by showing them the thought processes behind your own decisions. This will enable the team to make decisions that are in alignment with yours. The better the decisions made by you and your team, the quicker you will achieve your goals and Vision.

## example

A Vice President understood the value of making decisions based on the information available and of not wavering from the decision after making it. His decisions were extremely well thought-out and he had established a reputation for being an excellent decision-maker.

When asked how he was able to do this, he said, "The first thing I do is write down the problem and obtain every bit of pertinent information regarding it. Next, I come up with three possible solutions. I look at the pros and cons of each solution and think about how each outcome would affect the company, my team and myself in the short-, mid- and long-term. My last step is to decide on one of the three solutions and act on it."

He then went on to explain, "If I have more time, I write down the decision and put it in my desk drawer. After I have had a night to think about it, I review it. Most of the time I stick with my original decision although I do make adjustments about 25% of the time. Taking this time to let the answer resonate while I think it through allows me to be less emotional and more objective."

# 13 *be a* **REFLECTIVE** *thinker*

Every coach should develop the habit of reflective thinking. Looking at your past and using those experiences will help you succeed in the present and in the future. Being contemplative can pay off on a daily basis. End each day by reflecting on your activities in order to prepare yourself for the next day. You should do the same for each week, month, quarter and year.

Being reflective represents the lost art of thinking. By taking time out to contemplate, you can make reflective thinking a habit. Those individuals who have the ability to think seem to be a step ahead. They temporarily "stop time" while they reflect on ways to make their desired future become a reality.

Coaches who reflect on a daily basis rejuvenate themselves. They focus their attention on past events and reflect on how the events relate to their desired future. These coaches possess competence, security and wisdom. They understand that life is a thinking game.

**example**

Carl has been a front-line manager for 17 years and plans to maintain this position until he retires. He develops world-class professionals year in and year out. His team's outstanding results reflect his ability as a leader and coach. He's noted for weeding out low performers quickly and efficiently — keeping only the highest performing people on his team.

When asked how he has managed to do this year after year, he credits his reflective thinking time. At the end of every month, he schedules a one-hour appointment with himself. During this reflective time, he reviews each team player's performance and assesses their strengths and weaknesses. He than asks himself, "Would I hire a candidate with these characteristics?" If the answer is yes, he moves forward with this employee's development plan. If the answer is no, he immediately puts the employee on a corrective action plan that outlines the necessary adjustments to keep this player on the team. He continues this process until he has reviewed every one of his direct reports and determined the correct course of action for each.

This monthly reflection exercise of reviewing each team member's performance allows him to ensure his team is performing at its best. By reflecting on the past, he is able to succeed in the present and in the future.

# #14 **PATIENCE** is the quickest route to achieving goals

World-class chess players have the patience to think through every move. Similarly, the best coaches understand the value of patience. It takes time to build a solid infrastructure. It is important to take certain things slowly and have a long-term view of the future. Patience acts as an accelerator to achieving your goals and gives you the ability to pre-plan your success.

Teach your team the importance of this virtue by modeling patience. When a coach acts patiently, it builds confidence and a feeling of security among the team. Spend time on activities that slow things down. Coach your team members how to think through issues before taking action. Show them how to make every decision count. Teach them to wait for things to unfold completely. This will enable you and your team to do things right the first time in order to reach desired goals more quickly. Patience is a virtue that every coach must possess. Remember there are no shortcuts to being successful. It takes time; so relax and have the patience to know your desired result will materialize.

### example

Tom was very pleased about three new technical managers he had hired. He had high hopes for all of them but was especially looking forward to Nancy's performance since she had the most experience. Therefore, he was disappointed after 90 days when Nancy's team came in last in productivity. Tom scheduled a meeting with Nancy to discuss the situation. He began by asking if anything was wrong and if there was anything he could do to assist her. She said that everything was fine and she just needed more time with her team to produce the desired results. By the end of the meeting, Tom was confident that her department would continue to improve because she was executing the basic structure and discipline that he knew would drive performance.

After another 60 days, her team's productivity had increased but still didn't meet his expectations. Tom scheduled another meeting and asked Nancy to review her management style and methodology again. Nancy explained that she was patiently working the basics that would lead to building a long-term, high-performance team. Tom realized her approach had merit and decided to wait another three months before making a final decision regarding her abilities.

After three months had passed, Nancy's team had made tremendous leaps in productivity and achieved the #1 spot among the 12 teams reporting to Tom. In fact, Nancy's team held the top spot for 13 months in a row. It was a direct result of her being patient enough to build her team right the first time. Luckily, Tom's division was strong enough to support Nancy as she did this. Tom and Nancy's patience not only paid huge dividends to the company, it also resulted in promotions for them both—Tom moved into senior management and Nancy took Tom's position.

# #15 CULTIVATE
## a farm team

Some of your team members, including high performers, are not going to stay with you forever. That's why you need to spend at least four hours each month cultivating a farm team. You can use this team to replace players who are promoted or leave your company. You can't afford to wait until a vacancy occurs to start this process.

Cultivating a farm team is a proactive method of developing prospective employees. It provides you with the security of knowing that if you lose a team member, you can easily fill the position. To make this a reality, you need to set the goal, produce a plan, create action steps and record them in your daily planner. If you don't write it down, it may not happen.

The most important time to farm is when you are fully staffed. Don't wait for the crisis! Successful individuals aren't looking for a job — they already have one. Just running a newspaper ad doesn't always bring you the highest caliber of people. Think ahead, take your time and cultivate your farm team. When someone leaves, you have a ready pool of potential candidates.

**example**

A manager had recently experienced the crisis of having to fill several positions in his department at once. His top team member moved to another state and another team member had decided to go back to school. He had impending deadlines to meet and needed to recruit and hire replacements in an extremely short period of time.

After this experience, this manager decided to cultivate a farm team rather than deal with a similar situation in the future. He set a goal of finding one new player for his farm team each quarter. His plan was to conduct two interviews a month that would build relationships with prospective employees. In his daily planner, he outlined action steps which included calling prospects and interviewing them in person. He held himself accountable to confirming and conducting each appointment in order to reach his goal.

When an opening on his team came up eight months later, the manager had three great candidates from which to choose. He realized that cultivating a farm team is preventive maintenance. By consistently recruiting throughout the year, he minimized the stress and time it took to replace team members.

# Review #11 — #15

Though these coaching tips are familiar, the key is to learn, understand and internalize each of them. They should become an automatic and permanent part of your professional behavior. We've included the following review activity to help you.

First, identify the principle that corresponds to each illustration. Then, think about how you have used this principle in the past, or come up with a plan to put it into action in the future. This type of reflection activity will help you master each principle and easily implement it in your world. Have fun!

\# _____  _____

_____

**Action:** _____

_____

_____

_____


\# _____  _____

_____

**Action:** _____

_____

_____

_____

\# \_\_\_\_ _____

**Action:** _____

\# \_\_\_\_ _____

**Action:** _____

\# \_\_\_\_ _____

**Action:** _____

# #16 *make* **RAPID ADJUSTMENTS**
## *without losing balance*

As a coach, understand that you are often performing a balancing act between different and changing priorities. You must handle this chaos without becoming emotional or getting knocked off balance. To do this, be aware of your environment, trust your instincts, stay calm and remain true to your Vision and your plan to achieve it. This mindset will enable you to make rapid adjustments that will move the team forward. It will also help you evolve into a stronger, more effective coach.

When you maintain balance, you gain an unbelievable amount of energy. However, when you are knocked off course, you have to quickly get back on track. Simply refocus and make the needed adjustment. Do this by determining where you are and where you need to be. Learn from the experience and move on towards achieving your goals.

■ ■ ■ ■ ***example***

Felicia, a division manager of a moderately-sized company, loved her job. She supervised five managers who had a total of 50 employees reporting to them. She worked hard to build a strong team. This included holding weekly team meetings. One morning, she came to work at 7 a.m. prepared for her meeting. Not one of her team members came to work or called in. She started to panic but decided to wait a little longer before taking action.

By midday, she uncovered that a competitor had hired away her entire team. Shortly after that, her boss asked if she knew what was going on. He became angry and told Felicia that she needed to find a way to staff her division immediately. Although she was knocked off balance, she quickly started calling people. Fortunately, she had always believed in the importance of developing a "farm team" of prospective employees and had several potential replacements. By dinner, she had hired her first new manager who brought three people along with him and agreed to help find others.

It took nearly six months to get back to full strength. Felicia never looked back and didn't allow herself to lose balance again. She made the necessary adjustments as quickly as possible and built a strong team. In addition, she gained confidence as a result of her ability to rebuild after such a devastating event. Her achievement of rebuilding her division in just six months proved beyond a doubt that she could make rapid adjustments without losing balance.

# 17 REPETITION *creates desired habits*

Use repetition to train your team to get the job done correctly. There are many job skills that each employee needs to perform that may not come naturally. Therefore, set aside time to help them develop the necessary habits for success.

Show team members how to perform their jobs rather than just telling them how to do it. Role-play or "drill for skill" at every opportunity. Use repetition to make these habits a part of each team members' automatic behavior. Through repetition, you can etch the desired habit onto the walls of each person's mind.

Professional athletes, artists, musicians and scientists all master their skills through practice and repetition. This drives peak performance. The habits become a natural part of their behavior so that they don't even have to think to perform. In the same way, you want your team members to use practice and repetition to develop their skills to the highest possible level. Your primary job as a coach is to develop the correct habits your team members need to be successful. Just keep at it and remember that everyone has to grow both personally and professionally.

■ ■ ■ ■ **example**

A district manager took over a new territory that was ranked last out of 12 branches. After assessing the skill level of his management team, the district manager decided to institute a mandatory program of scheduling weekly One-on-One meetings with his store managers. He knew that these meetings would move them out of the "twelfth place." Each meeting included role play and "drill for skill" activities that would drive proactive behavior. Through consistent repetition of conducting One-on-One meetings, his district moved into fifth place within eight months.

# 18 *KNOW* *your competition*

You must know who your competitors are. This information affects how you position yourself in the marketplace. It also enables you to highlight your company's strengths against the competition and take full advantage of what your company does best. Many times, this is the difference between success and failure.

Every person who works for you expects you to have information regarding your company's competitive advantage. They look to you as the expert. This information will help them be creative and innovative in their positions. It also gives team members an overall view of how their position can affect these advantages. Be aware of what your competition lacks in the market and focus on those needs. Even a little difference can make a big impact. The more you know about your competition, the better your chance of success.

Spend time researching your competition. Visit trade shows and retail outlets and observe what the competition is doing now and what they have planned for the future. Read industry publications to stay on the leading edge of what those in your industry are doing. By doing this consistently, you will be able to show your team members exactly what your company needs to be dominant in the marketplace. Model this behavior and build a team of industry experts.

■ ■ ■ ■ **example**

The Chief Technical Officer (CTO) of a large software manufacturing company held monthly team meetings where he provided tips to increase productivity as well as discussed topics suggested by his team members. The CTO was continually looking for new topics for future meetings. During one team meeting, a team member asked a question about the company's competitors. As the CTO answered his question, he realized that discussing competitor-related matters with his team could positively impact productivity.

At each team meeting he dedicated 15 minutes to providing updates about the competition. Little by little, each team member started thinking of ways to take advantage of their company's competitive edge. Some team members suggested ways they could develop their positions and departments; others had suggestions on how to beat the competition using innovative new strategies. Each team member was actively looking for ways to improve and was more motivated to perform his/her role. By knowing their competition, each team was able to contribute and achieve unprecedented success. The CTO realized that knowing your competition helps you to build a high-performance team.

# 19 *understand that people do things for* **THEIR REASONS**, *not yours*

Always keep in mind that people work for themselves first and foremost. Most people work not because they love to work — they work to survive and to pay for their dreams.

Team members will maximize their effort because they are working for themselves and their future. Their job is simply a vehicle to get them there. If you know what your team members want in the short- and long-term, you can show them how the company can become the vehicle to achieving their future goals. This creates a powerful alignment between the company and the employee.

Have each team member determine his/her Vision encompassing both personal and professional goals. This represents the team member's key motivations and largest energy source. Team members need to be able to tap into this energy pool in order to stay focused on their high-payoff activities.

Learn to talk each employee's "language" by speaking the words they used to describe their Vision. Understand what's important to each of your team members and show them how their jobs can help them achieve their dreams. This will increase job satisfaction and productivity, resulting in success for the entire team.

■ ■ ■ ■ **example**

Jeff, an Account Executive, came into his manager's office and announced that he could no longer perform his job. He felt burned out and the job wasn't right for him. The manager disagreed and asked Jeff to take out the Vision statement he had written at the beginning of the year. His Vision included both his personal and business goals.

As Jeff and his manager discussed Jeff's Vision, they uncovered numerous ways of how his current position and future career path would lead him to achieve his desired goals. The manager also challenged Jeff to think about other ways the company could become the vehicle to achieve this Vision.

Jeff realized he had never truly understood the connection between what he wanted and how the company could get him there. The exercise made him realize that the company could take him to his desired future state. He became more motivated and experienced consistent results because he was doing things for his reasons, not the company's.

# #20 *spend* **ONE-ON-ONE** *time with each team member*

A coach's primary responsibility is to grow and develop his/her team members to achieve their next level of performance. To do this successfully, spend One-on-One time with each team member on a regular basis. This allows you to provide your team members with professional direction that will lead to increased productivity and results.

It is important that you prioritize your day to make time for this personal attention. Face-to-face time is best. But if you're managing from a distance and don't have that opportunity, the telephone is the second best alternative. Schedule One-on-One time with each team member on a weekly basis if possible. If not, meet monthly. Be prepared—plan ahead, have an agenda and determine your professional development objectives for the meeting. Inform team members that this is the opportunity to focus on their development, not housekeeping issues.

One-on-One meetings build the skill sets and the professional maturity individuals need to reach their next level of performance. If you don't spend time developing your team members, they will eventually leave you for an organization that will. Use this One-on-One time to talk about the team member's world. Then, challenge your team members to develop the habits that will take them and the company to their next higher level. By dedicating time to your team members you will form lasting partnerships and will be better able to keep them motivated and focused. Impactful coaches pull their team members through the knotholes of life. This exercise better equips them to succeed by helping them realize the reality of their situation.

■ ■ ■ ■ **example**

A new manager had been at a company for four months and was not performing successfully. There was high turnover in his department, little loyalty to either him or the company and low productivity. He felt that his team members took up too much of his time and prevented him from performing his other responsibilities. He was so frustrated that he approached his boss to discuss the situation. He asked her to help him determine what he was doing wrong so that he could get his team on track.

She asked some questions and uncovered that the only time he met One-on-One with his team members was to discuss housekeeping issues, productivity levels and corrective action plans. He didn't interact with his employees unless they were doing something wrong. She offered him the following simple advice: "Spend time with your team members. You can't do the job alone. Take the time to educate and develop them. Inspire, engage and challenge them. All winning coaches develop the skill levels of their team members and you can do the same."

The manager took her advice even though it was outside of his comfort zone. Over the next five months, he met One-on-One with his team members weekly. He realized that spending time to grow and develop his team members was making a difference. The role-playing and "drill for skill" activities he used during these meetings to improve specific skills drove productivity up, and increased job satisfaction.

# Review #16 — #20

Though these coaching tips are familiar, the key is to learn, understand and internalize each of them. They should become an automatic and permanent part of your professional behavior. We've included the following review activity to help you.

First, identify the principle that corresponds to each illustration. Then, think about how you have used this principle in the past, or come up with a plan to put it into action in the future. This type of reflection activity will help you master each principle and easily implement it in your world. Have fun!

\# \_\_\_\_\_ _____

_____

**Action:** _____

_____

_____

_____

\# \_\_\_\_\_ _____

_____

**Action:** _____

_____

_____

_____

**#** _____ _____

_____

**Action:** _____

_____

_____

_____

**#** _____ _____

_____

**Action:** _____

_____

_____

_____

**#** _____ _____

_____

**Action:** _____

_____

_____

_____

# 21 create a culture of "NO FEAR"

To remain competitive in today's environment, you need to create a culture of "no fear" within your team. "No fear" means having the freedom to bring forth ideas and honesty in a world of structure and discipline. This will open the door to creativity and innovation, and enable you to build a high-performance team. Team members are motivated in an atmosphere of "no fear." They are not scared to take calculated risks and the environment supports them in simply being themselves. This enables the coach to help them achieve their potential sooner.

Most people think that making a mistake is a sign of weakness — and fear management's repercussions in doing so. Help them understand that admitting mistakes, shortcomings and a lack of knowledge demonstrates strength. All issues are simply a part of day-to-day business and should be viewed as instruments of learning and opportunities for growth.

Teach your team members the advantages of working in a culture of "no fear." These benefits include increased productivity, rapid adjustments in decision-making, increased morale and accelerated professional and personal growth. In addition, your team members will take more calculated risks in this type of environment which will allow you to move your business forward. This culture empowers your team members while maintaining the positive stress of respect.

■ ■ ■ ■ **example**

In a highly visible brokerage firm, there was a manager who did not allow her people to make mistakes. She was so adamant about this that her team members were reluctant to admit even the smallest of errors. When one team member made a $3 data entry error, he decided to keep quiet about it. Three months later, the mistake surfaced and ended up costing the company many thousands of dollars.

At that point, the auditing department got involved and found incorrect data entries were made many times by different employees within the same department. Though the employees thought they would be fired for their mistakes, the manager was dehired and the company realized that building the correct culture greatly affects the bottom line. As a result, this situation became a case study for the entire company. All managers are now encouraged to build a culture of "no fear" where mistakes are a part of doing business. They teach their team members to acknowledge mistakes, learn from them and move on.

# 22 communication must be built on a foundation of CONFLUENCY

You must build professional relationships where everyone accepts responsibility for communicating clearly and honestly. Coach your team members to come together to express their feelings, thoughts and opinions. By letting them know that you will do the same, you will create a unified approach to achieve common objectives. The agreed-upon message is: We respect each other as individuals. Therefore, we can talk openly about each other's <u>professional behavior</u> and not compromise our relationship.

When you observe behavior that needs to be addressed, talk to the team member in private as soon as possible. This type of confluent communication creates an environment that allows people to be themselves. There are no hidden agendas — everyone knows where he or she stands. As a result, team members feel safe enough to take risks and continually learn. Don't only use this technique when there are problems. Instead, make confluent communication a habit by practicing it continually. If you communicate confluently during good and bad times, you will experience positive outcomes, build loyalty among your team and support the culture of "no fear."

■ ■ ■ ■ **example**

Robert, The manager of a 20-person unit was working extremely long hours, 7 day a week. However, he was not getting the desired results from team members — and this impacted the company's bottom line. The Vice President examined the situation and chose to communicate confluently with Robert.

"Robert, you know I value you as an employee, but I need to speak to you about your professional behavior. I know you're working hard and your work ethic is excellent, but your ability to get results from team members is unsatisfactory at the present time. Is this is an accurate assessment?"

"Yes, I just can't seem to get control of my workload. I seem to be running inside a hamster cage — the faster I run, the further away I move from what I want to accomplish. It's really frustrating to me."

"Well, Robert, are you willing to make the necessary changes to get back your control?"

"Yes."

"OK, let's start by developing a plan to leverage your strengths. Let's look at your job description and project list to see what we can eliminate or delegate. This will give you more time to work on your high-payoff activities. How does that sound, Robert?"

"Great, I'll re-work my schedule according to our plan and share it with you by tomorrow morning. I truly appreciate you supporting me through this tough time."

This confluent conversation enabled Robert to get back on track — boosting company profits.

# 23 S.O.S.
## (Separation of Space)

When life becomes too much for you to handle, don't panic. Instead, send out an S.O.S.! Separation of Space is a visualization exercise that creates space between a crisis situation and one's emotional behavior. It is usually during crisis situations when professionals become reactive and make mistakes. That's why taking the time to S.O.S. will help you become more successful.

When you feel your emotions rising in a situation, stop and take a breath. Then, mentally separate the situation from your emotions. This will decrease your stress level while enabling you to gain control of your emotions. It also keeps you centered and allows you to make more objective decisions. By not allowing your emotions to affect your decisions, you will think clearly. S.O.S. helps you perform in a proactive state so that you can do more in less time.

Coaches need to model this behavior to their team. By doing so, the team learns how to maintain composure while under fire, make effective decisions quickly and handle any situation professionally. The ability to S.O.S. leads to increased results, confidence and job satisfaction. It's an ideal approach for conflict resolution.

A group of 15 scientists had been working on a project for 18 months. During this time, they had developed a prototype for a new product. The project leader was excited because he had met the objectives set by the group that funded the project. However, at the end of the 18 months he was told, "I know you accomplished everything we asked for but we modified our design. Now we need you to redesign 50% of the prototype within 3 weeks."

At that point, the project leader could have gone back to his team frustrated and told them the new assignment was impossible. Instead, he used S.O.S. and proactively reviewed the situation. He determined that if everyone agreed to work alternate 12-hour shifts over the next three weeks, the goal could be met. He remained objective, kept his emotions at bay and transferred this calmness to his team.

He continued to S.O.S. each day in order to keep his stress away from the team. He knew that if he allowed his emotions to join with the reality of the seemingly impossible deadline, the team would never achieve the goal. He stayed calm and objective by constantly "S.O.S.ing" and maintaining focus on the goal. His team worked the 12-hour shifts a day and actually managed to beat the deadline. The project leader's ability to S.O.S. kept the entire team on track and earned them special recognition for their outstanding efforts.

# 24 LISTEN to the data your team members give you

Winning coaches have all of their senses working together to pick up on the information transmitted to them. All verbal, non-verbal, and written communication — even omissions and silence — are an endless source of information. Subtle clues are connected to much larger issues. Your job as a coach is to be sensitive and inquisitive about the meaning of these subtle hints. Then, trend the data received from each team member to help you coach, challenge and develop your team on an individual basis. Trending allows you to see patterns of behavior and provides you with a greater understanding of the meaning behind individual pieces of information.

Use this data to assess the reality of each team member's abilities, strengths, weaknesses, and level of job satisfaction. Look for signs of frustration, boredom or happiness. Continue to pay attention to the data your team members give and make adjustments as needed. This data allows you to build customized plans to release each team member's total human potential.

A manager was sitting in her office on the last Friday of the month reviewing her team's results. Her top producer came in with an order that put her at 300% of quota for the second month in a row. The manager was ecstatic and suggested to her that they go out and celebrate. The team member shook her head and simply said with her eyes looking at the floor, "Do you mind if I close the door?" The manager's heart sank because she knew that something was wrong.

The manager asked, "What can I help you with?" The top producer responded by saying, "I've been leaving you hints about how unhappy I am for months. I brought up service issues at several sales meetings, and I personally asked for your help regarding these concerns nearly a year ago. It seems as if you only care about my results." The top producer then handed the manager her resignation letter. The manager asked if anything could persuade her to stay. The top producer replied, "Remember the other day when I told you how frustrated I was with the way our support team is handling my customers? You told me not to worry because it would get better. You've been telling me that for nearly 11 months. You know I sell the company with my reputation. I can't stay here knowing that my customers aren't being treated the way in which I promise. I feel like you don't listen to me and I can no longer work for you."

The manager lost her top producer because she didn't listen to the information this team member provided her both in verbal communication and subtle hints. The loss of a key player on the team greatly affected the manager and the company and provided a tough lesson.

# 25 TEACH *your team to fish*
## *(solve their own problems)*

As the saying goes, feed a man a fish and he can eat for a day; teach a man to fish and he can eat for a lifetime. Keep this in mind and teach your team to be self-sufficient by showing them how to achieve their desired goals.

The difference between a great coach and a mediocre coach is that a great coach <u>shows</u> team members how to do their jobs while a mediocre coach simply <u>tells</u> them. Build a high-performance team by showing your team members how to do what you expect. Don't assume anything. Confirm what they can and can't do to uncover their strengths and weaknesses. Then, leverage their strengths and improve their weaknesses to enable them to become self-sufficient.

Confirm that each team member understands what you expect by monitoring their actions. Help them make the necessary adjustments. By teaching your team members how to do their job correctly the first time, you'll save hundreds of hours. You can also be away from your team and know that the desired end result will occur. Teach your team to solve their own problems so you have the time to strategize and lead.

**example**

A Sales Manager, Aaron, was put in charge of developing a new sales team. He hired people with sales experience, gave them a territory, product and industry information and told them to go out and sell. He said, "Go hit the pavement — you'll do great." He just assumed that their sales experience would enable them to sell his product line and services.

The turnover rate among his employees was high. No one was reaching quota, and his boss told him that if things didn't improve, he would be out of a job.

Aaron reviewed the situation and concluded that his sales team needed more training. He decided to demonstrate to his team members exactly how to do their jobs before sending them out to sell. He went into the field with them and showed them how to get in front of their prospects, how to position the products, how to qualify, how to close, and how to service each account. He equipped these sales veterans with selling tips that worked for his product line. Once they started selling, their results went through the roof and Aaron was able to remain in his position. He also learned a valuable lesson: in order to get people to do a job right, they have to be taught exactly how it should be done. He taught his team how to fish and the results were well worth it!

# Review #21 — #25

Though these coaching tips are familiar, the key is to learn, understand and internalize each of them. They should become an automatic and permanent part of your professional behavior. We've included the following review activity to help you.

First, identify the principle that corresponds to each illustration. Then, think about how you have used this principle in the past, or come up with a plan to put it into action in the future. This type of reflection activity will help you master each principle and easily implement it in your world. Have fun!

\# _____ _____

_____

**Action:** _____

_____

_____

_____

\# _____ _____

_____

**Action:** _____

_____

_____

_____

\# \_\_\_\_ _____

_____

**Action:** _____

_____

_____

_____

\# \_\_\_\_ _____

_____

**Action:** _____

_____

_____

_____

\# \_\_\_\_ _____

_____

**Action:** _____

_____

_____

_____

# 26 LOOK BEHIND questions
## to uncover your team members' skill level

Your experience enables you to determine the level of questions your team members should be asking. It is important to be conscious of these questions because you need to know what to expect from each team member. The questions they ask reveal who they are, their level of skill/competency and their depth of understanding about their job.

If their questions do not meet your expectations, use this as an opportunity to develop their skill level. Also take an objective look at whether the individual will reach the skill level needed to perform their job. If team members are asking the right questions, praise them and encourage them to ask more questions. These inquiries tell you how to coach them to their next level of proficiency by defining their current skill level. If team members aren't asking the right questions, work with them to find out why. Then, help them develop their skills or find another position better-suited to their abilities.

■ ■ ■ ■ **example**

A new Office Manager was hired to control all expenses of a small business. He showed tremendous desire but continued to ask basic accounting questions.

In this situation, the coach did four things.
1. He asked: "What has changed between the interview process and now? You said you could perform the duties of the job but it's apparent through your questions that you are not at the skill level outlined in the job description."
2. The coach then assessed the team member's TRUE skill level and received his agreement. "We both agree that your abilities are at a beginner's level and the position requires more advanced-level knowledge."
3. Together, they created a plan outlining adjustments and a skill level needed to perform his job duties.
   "Here's the plan: We will train you on skills necessary to perform the job successfully. The expense report must be completed by October 1. Projections must be completed by October 10. Collections must be at 95% by October 15. We will meet twice a month to check your progress. In addition, accuracy is critical. Make sure you double-check your work."
4. The coach then held the Office Manager accountable. The coach correctly assumed that the Office Manager's actions would show whether he could perform the job successfully. As it turned out, the Office Manager wasn't able to fulfill the job duties and had to leave the position.

# 27 **PRAISE** *progress*

Looking for a way to motivate your team members? Would you like to increase their job satisfaction? Here's an easy way to do both at the same time. Praise progress of any kind.

Don't wait to let people know how well they are doing — instead, praise progress as it occurs. Be aware of your team members' actions, both large and small. Then, praise them for accomplishments of any size that have a positive impact on the team. Tell them what you think of their performance in a timely manner. You can also praise a team member's performance by passing-on what co-workers, vendors and clients say. Everyone enjoys knowing they've done a task well. Even if you think your team members know you appreciate their efforts, say it! They need to hear it from you.

Praise is extremely rewarding and motivating to team members. It can be simple — a handshake, words of encouragement or any other type of positive attention. Unfortunately, most managers are too busy to stop and give praise. Most managers believe that team members who are doing well know this and don't need to be recognized. There's nothing less motivating than continually achieving without recognition. Every team member wants and needs to know when they're doing well. Don't forget to praise progress — it pays off for everyone!

**example**

Ken is a manager with a great team of highly-motivated and talented individuals. The business environment was extremely positive and the team was busily working to develop exciting products. They had aggressive goals and production schedules that they had no trouble meeting. Everyone was doing well, feeling good about their achievements and looking forward to the next project.

Although the team members seemed happy, the team unfortunately experienced a 50% turnover rate within an 18-month period. Ken decided to survey his team to determine why so many people were leaving. He found the main reason for high turnover was that his team members never felt their efforts were appreciated. They didn't mind working hard, but they expected to be noticed occasionally for their dedication.

From that point on, Ken deliberately took time during and after each project to reflect on individual and team successes. He also handed out awards of recognition before moving the team on to the next project. In a short period of time, turnover decreased to 10%. The team members were motivated and satisfied in their positions because their accomplishments were being recognized on a regular basis.

## create
# PEOPLE POWER

You can't do it alone. As a coach, you must be conscious of the power of working with others and use it to produce results that wouldn't otherwise occur. Recognize that the answers to most problems your business faces actually lie within your team members.

When you and a team member address a specific issue together, you will often create a solution that wouldn't have been reached if you were each working alone. This is "People Power!" It can only happen when two or more people are working in the same direction toward a common Vision or goal. When "People Power" occurs, you can almost see the idea come alive in the form of a light bulb above the heads of those who created it. Basically, when people come together, it releases an untapped source of energy. To do this most effectively, the individuals involved should just relax and keep the ideas coming.

Model this brainstorming process for your team members. Encourage team members to rely on each other's input, experience and creativity. The mark of a high-performance team is the ability to use "People Power" at will.

**example**

A company was launching a new product. Their two product developers had been trying to come up with a name for the product for nearly six months. Both created their own list. Then, they met and started sharing their ideas. They were not satisfied with any of the names on their lists and tried to come up with a satisfactory name by working together.

After an uneventful hour, the receptionist notified one of the individuals that he had a delivery downstairs. The product developers decided to take a break and went down to the lobby together to pick up the delivery. As they waited to take the elevator back upstairs, they relaxed their minds and just stared at the elevator doors without talking. As the doors opened, they turned to each other simultaneously and began talking. It was as though a bottle of champagne had been uncorked — they heard the pop and the ideas just flowed. This conversation led them to the name they had been trying to come up with for the product. Both individuals shared in its creation and felt extreme satisfaction at the outcome. "People Power" helped create the perfect name for their product.

# 29 NEVER SAY
## "If I were you..."

As soon as you say, "If I were you..." your team members usually stop listening to anything that follows that statement. You aren't them — they know it and you know it. You don't have the same issues, relationships, pressures or experiences. This phrase automatically elicits a negative response.

Instead of risking this reaction, use examples based on your experience but phrase them in a way that sounds like you learned or observed the behavior from someone else. For example, "Tara, I remember a guy that I used to work with that once had this same problem. Would you be interested in knowing how he resolved this issue?" This gets the same point across in a manner that will be accepted and respected by the team. It is also more likely that the team will implement your suggestions as a result.

The only time it is okay to say, "If I were you...," is if a team member asks you specifically for this type of advice. Confirm that they are asking for an example of how you handled a similar situation and then provide it to them. Be sure to also ask how they plan to use your experience and knowledge in their current situation. This gives them control over how they will adapt your suggestion and makes them feel like a partner in the decision rather than a subordinate.

Early in her management career, Tracy always used the phrase, "If I were you..." because she knew she was an outstanding professional in her field. She felt she could increase results by telling people to perform their jobs the way she had performed hers. Instead, she noticed that as she kept giving the team "I" answers, she was pushing them further away.

The team members didn't want to be Tracy; they wanted to be themselves. They would politely listen to Tracy but rarely implemented her suggestions. After several months, she pulled one of her top performers aside and asked him why the team members were resistant to her ideas. He told her that they were simply tired of hearing about her successes.

She decided she needed to try a different approach. Instead of sharing stories about how she did things well, she started taking the time to better understand her team members (who they are personally, how they want to be communicated with, etc.). She also taught them to discover solutions on their own using creativity and innovation, and helped team members to think on their own. This gave the team members a stronger sense of achievement and more control over their results.

# 30 compare ACTIONS to words to determine REALITY

Look... listen... compare... and be amazed by what you'll learn. To be an effective coach, you must constantly uncover and deal with reality. The best way to do this is to match your team members' _actions_ to their _words_. Why? Because words can often create an illusion while actions reflect the individual's true level of commitment. You need to deal with reality in order to create the correct customized plan for each individual that will accelerate their productivity and release total human potential.

This is an easy principle to immediately put to use. Just view life as if it were a silent movie. Watch the actions of the individuals on your team. If their actions don't equal their words, reconfirm whether their goal is still desired. If it is, then help the team member make adjustments and motivate him/her to get back on track. If it isn't, eliminate the goal and create a new one that represents reality.

An individual's actions over time demonstrate what they truly believe. Their actions/trends will tell the story of who they are, what they want and how much they are willing to do to get there.

■ ■ ■ ■ **example**

A manager assigned Eileen a project and reviewed the pertinent information with her. Eileen discussed a timeline with the manager and agreed to complete the project by the end of the week. When her manager checked her status in the middle of the week, Eileen wasn't even close to achieving her goal. The manager realized this was an excellent opportunity to compare her actions with her words to uncover her reality.

The reality was that Eileen was not acting as if she wanted to accomplish the goal. Did she overcommit? Did she not communicate honestly? Did someone she was counting on let her down? The manager looked at Eileen's actions and used them as a mirror to help Eileen assess her behavior and make the necessary adjustments. This included her thoughts, emotions and commitment needed to reach her goals. Eileen's learning was accelerated because she couldn't argue with the reality she saw reflected in her own actions. She realized that she had too many deadlines to meet during the week and asked her manager to help her adjust the expectations.

The manager simply pointed out the difference between Eileen's words and actions to reveal the reality of the situation. This method will work the majority of the time for you and your team members. When it doesn't work, it usually means your team member is in denial. Don't give up! Keep on comparing their actions to their words and they will eventually see reality.

# Review #26 — #30

Though these coaching tips are familiar, the key is to learn, understand and internalize each of them. They should become an automatic and permanent part of your professional behavior. We've included the following review activity to help you.

First, identify the principle that corresponds to each illustration. Then, think about how you have used this principle in the past, or come up with a plan to put it into action in the future. This type of reflection activity will help you master each principle and easily implement it in your world. Have fun!

\# _____ _____

_____

**Action:** _____

_____

_____

_____

\# _____ _____

_____

**Action:** _____

_____

_____

_____

\# \_\_\_\_ _____

_____

**Action:** _____

_____

_____

_____

\# \_\_\_\_ _____

_____

**Action:** _____

_____

_____

_____

\# \_\_\_\_ _____

_____

**Action:** _____

_____

_____

_____

# Create your own

Congratulations, coach! You now have the information you need to take your team to the next level and achieve even greater success.

That's why I've provided space on the next few pages for you to record and share some of your own coaching principles. There's room for a title, definition and real-world example of how you have used your tip in the past or plan to use it in the future. I've also included an illustration of my own as proof that you don't need to be an artist to complete this exercise!

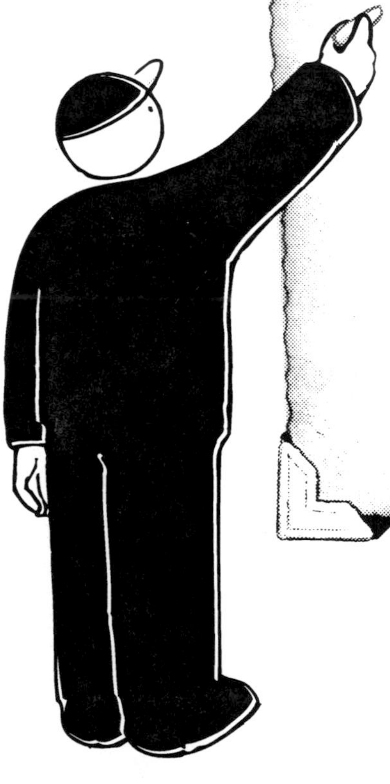

Please feel free to send in copies of the principles you create. You could possibly be featured in one of my next publications.

Mark David, President
The Mark David Corporation
411 Borel Avenue, Suite 504
San Mateo, CA 94402
800-410-ANSR (2677)
I can also be reached at **mark@markdavid.com**

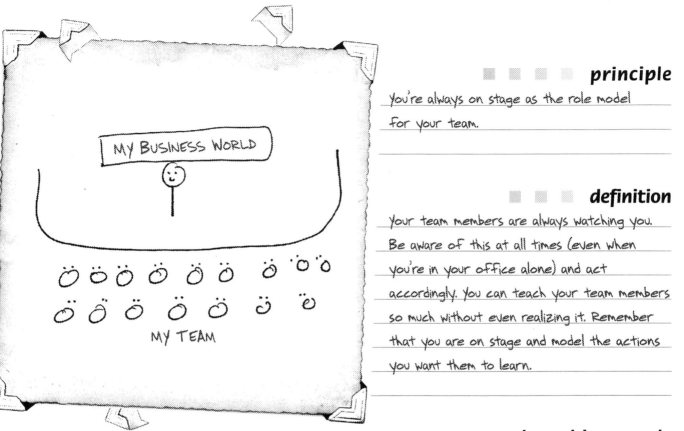

You're always on stage as the role model
for your team.

Your team members are always watching you.
Be aware of this at all times (even when
you're in your office alone) and act
accordingly. You can teach your team members
so much without even realizing it. Remember
that you are on stage and model the actions
you want them to learn.

I worked with one of my Sales Professionals to develop a proposal for a prospect whose business
would take our company to a whole new level. We submitted the contract and got the account! But
when we reviewed the contract, we realized we had forgotten to add in a very expensive financial item.
The Sales Professional begged me to absorb the amount but I refused since I knew our service was
worth the price. I decided to call the client and explain the situation. They realized we had made an
honest mistake and allowed the change. I had acted as a role model – my Sales Professional learned
from this and became a role model to the other members of the team as a result.

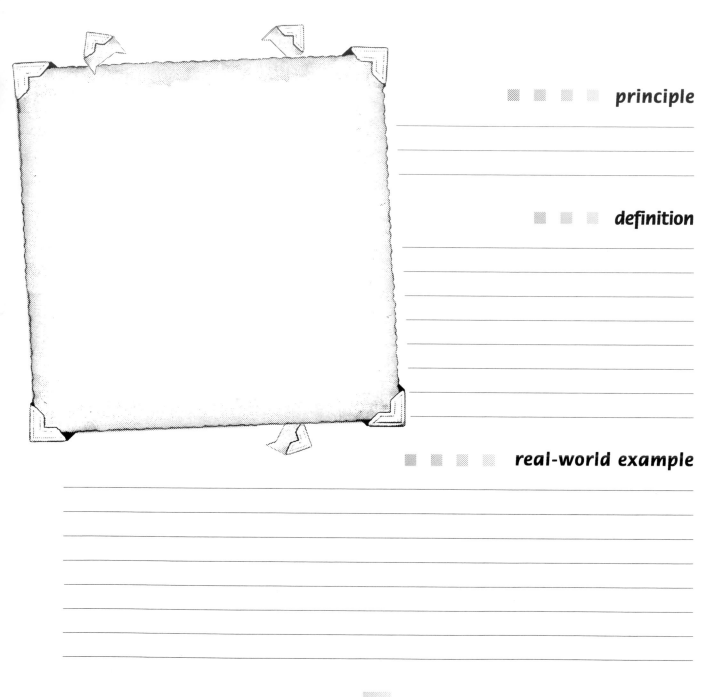

**principle**

**definition**

**real-world example**

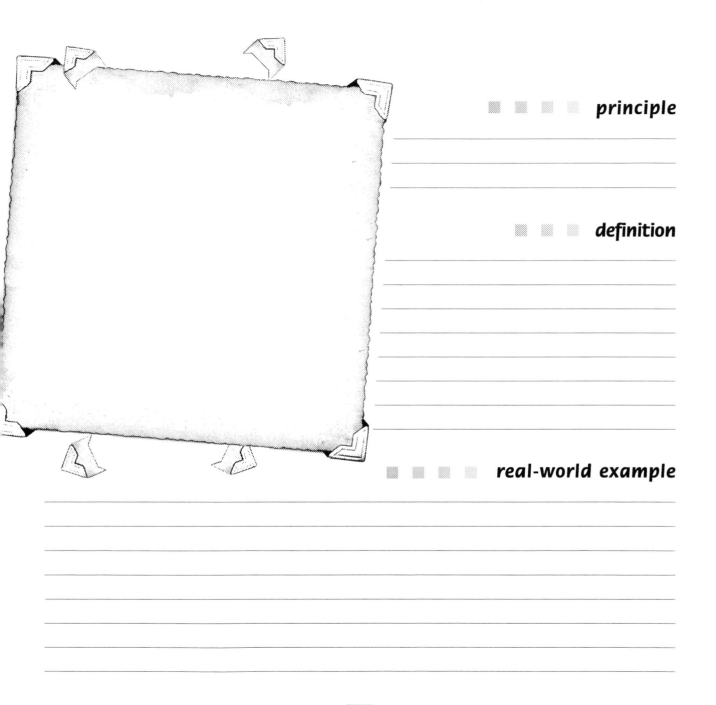

**principle**

**definition**

**real-world example**

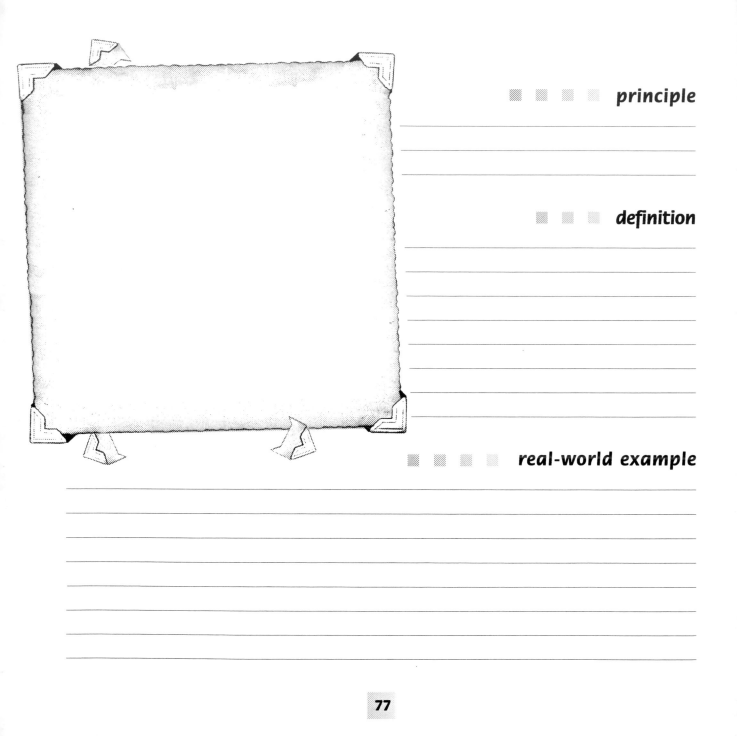

**principle**

**definition**

**real-world example**

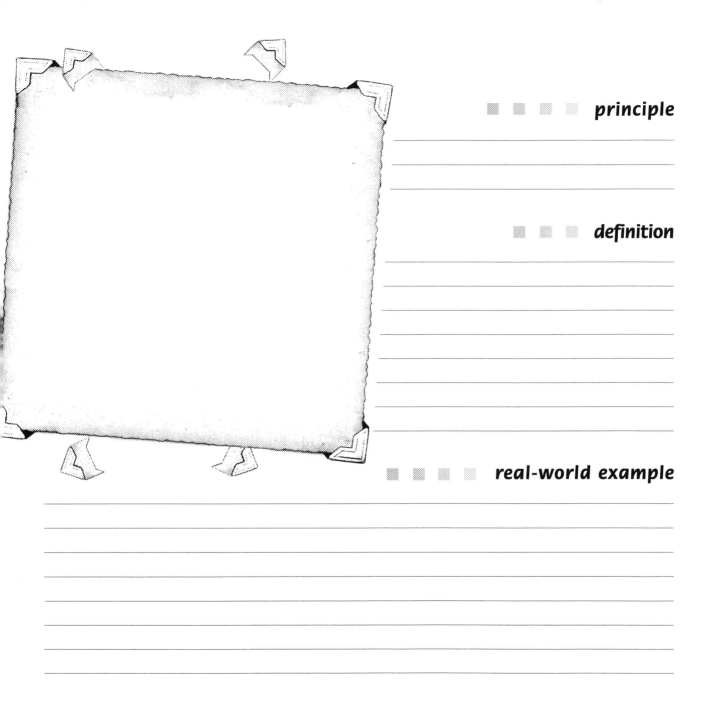

**principle**

**definition**

**real-world example**

# Also by Mark David

# TOOLS

## Human Development

Self-Manager Development Program

Personal Business Plan

Eye Chart Focusing Program

Habit Cards

- Customize Your Own
- Prospect One Hour a Day
- Ask for a Referral
- S.O.S

HUMANation® Tools Binder (includes the four tools listed above)

Coach Approach Program

Coach's Calendar

## Sales

Strategic Note Activity Pad

S.N.A.P. CD — Template

Crisis Anticipation Pad

Client Physical

Account Development Planner

# Also ...

# WORKSHOPS

HUMANation® Coach Approach

HUMANation® Tools

High-Probability Sales

Cellular Retail Sales

1-Day Tool Workshops (offered for all of the tools listed above)

# SERVICES

Certification Programs — Right-to-Train Licensing

Right-to-Reproduce Licensing

Customized Program Development

One-on-One Coaching

For more information, give us a call:

The Mark David Corporation @ 800-410-ANSR (2677)

411 Borel Avenue, Suite 504

San Mateo, CA 94402

Fax: 650-341-9906

Email: mark@markdavid.com